HOLDING OUT THE HAND OF A DEAD RELATIVE

HOLDING OUT THE HAND OF A DEAD RELATIVE

Poems

Ron Jost

Great Horned Publishing

Cover and book design by Great Horned Publishing

Cover image copyright © Henk van Rensbergen, abandoned-places.com

Third Edition

Printed in the United States of America

ISBN: 978-0-578-05246-5

Great Horned Publishing

More good stuff at GreatHornedPublishing.com

For C, O

Contents

V. VENUS FLYTRAPS

VI. LATTER DAYS

The Importance of Where the Comma Is Placed

Imagine being alive but unable to move of your own volition,
breezes, your branches creaking gently –
birds singing something sentimental
in the crook of your neck sends shivers down your trunk.
      Moisture coursing up
through your pulp and out into your thin, supple leaves,
      which relinquish it
to the sun's greedy rays after drinking long of it.
Imagine a female squirrel going down on you,
her little claws barely registering their clutch on your bark
      before scampering on
           to the next clutch,
and the next and the next and the next, until the last –
      she disappears finally
           into the underbrush.
The woodpecker at it so long it's ceased to be sound, you're wishing
      for the prickled pain
           you cannot feel.

How sad is love you will never know.
How sad is love, you will never know.

How real my love, transformed into a tree from corpse-seed (I will be) –
      a plot, some rain, strong roots
to break the surface of mud (all I need). And I will never drift away.
      I will sway.
Sing that song again, the only one I know, you birds. Me, providing shade
      for future shades –
you laughing persons holding hands, lying beneath my immense branches,
      telling secrets.

I. EMO KIDS

Lynch (1999)

The Baptist minister from Alabama
sits in his compound room in Louisville,
near midnight now.
                        Smokes pot
and contemplates the divinity of amorous feelings,
the way music throbs in the voice
when he sings it softly alive.

How the resonating air above his upturned mouth
forms a sort of net to trap the night.

How God is the throbbing, the resonating.
How our bodies resonate and throb.

And why separate it?

Let's trap it down here with us
and keep it going like radio beams
cocooning the ground at night.

The fact that is light.

"Let us all get lit now,"
he would preach in the ultimate church.
"Aren't we all life? Lift?"

My Father Hid His Face

I have been building my life out of
distorted fragments. How do you focus
a memory in the present if you weren't paying attention
to begin with? My father hid his face
when I wasn't looking. Now that I look I see
my father hides his face anyway. I am
lonely. I wear clothes that don't fit me. Hurry,
I don't have long to take you in before you're gone.
My son, am I smiling? Does the mystery nearly make you want to
hang it up? You will miss your puppy in 85 years. His black fur
will come back to you in confused patches, but it will still shine
          in the light
the way it does now when it is evening and the sun comes obliquely
through the living room window. Take it in, take us in, and don't let us go.

Acorn Drops, Candied Apples

One time the cops got called on me. You see
I broke a few things – a mirror an apple a guitar
two pairs of horn-rimmed glasses.

And also something broke inside of me.
The apple reflected in a shattered mirror.
A lyre played by two pairs of bloody Q-Tips
decked out for four ears.
                              That night a liar was born
that I kill now in this poem. In California
the acorns weighed different in my up-turned palm
from how they rested in Ohio as a child. For that
the cops got called on me.
                              The eyes are the first organ
to grow old. Dental records swear by the endurance
of teeth.
          A reversed image of the apple lingers in the dark glass
of the snake's phosphorescent eyes, a clenched hand radiates.

The police sketch artist approximates what the dead child
would've looked like if he hadn't been strangled long ago.
The sketch artist's projection is all that's left of our hope.
Could the cop've predicted 20 years ago my head sealed like
a candied apple? Or that I'd cut these tears free from their strings
off my fingertips only to have fingerprints to look forward to?

Drawing opening hands leads to the path upon which
          we become unchangingly new.

A Short History of Depression

– O

When my God-given little one
became a little bit
older, he began to ask questions that
got to be increasingly difficult
to answer, such as
how many trilobites does it take to make
a human? – and why are you crying so hard?

I didn't have the heart to . . .
                              I don't have the heart.

When one day my God-given little one
looks up to discover himself
with his own God-given little one, I will tell him
do what your daddy did and does
and pretend everything is okay for the sake
of all the other God-given little ones who are still to come.

Festivities of a Thursday Evening

Please God help me see why
it's not unusual
Thursday evening speeds by
watching video clips

Fifteen men take turns stepping up onto
a tree stump
while a single woman spends just enough time
halfway up a step ladder
making subtle motions side to side
with her head
slight adjustments of her sappy tongue
to receive from each man a million tiny seedlings
that will never take root

Her hands tied behind her back
by a producer who worried the straps
weren't tight enough

Sunlight reflects off a guy's wristwatch
until the cameraman adjusts his angle of approach

It was not the woman blinded by the glare
but still she is thankful for the adjustment

She is not being paid by the hour

The first man tripped dismounting the stump
the next one pretended the same what a clown
the last surely will be more careful on his way down

My mother was not there
but my father was
as was your daughter

Our Lawns, Our Beers

When taking their kids to the playground my neighbors walk
down the other side of the street so they won't need to stop

and speak with me – twitching in my shitty lawn chair, sitting in it
        on the brown lawn –
about the weather or the latest teen idol's latest pregnancy-
        instigated breakdown.

I am flattered to call my wife's mouth one of my many homes.
She calls me home for dinner and a tug of war ensues, foam

splashing on a platter the size of a dime. If it keeps on raining we will
        move south
and spend some time wearing shoes the color of tears. Our brewers
        are proud

of the consistency and potency of the many varieties of beer
        that they produce.
None of them calm the twitching, though, none of them capable
        of seducing me

into a smile that will last longer than the recollection
        of no one knows why
we are here. Nothing knows that we are here. Nothing knows
        nothing,
up in the sky.

To the Left

Everything she owned was packed
in a single cardboard box
which ended up sitting
overnight
in a puddle outside the shelter. The next morning
no matter how she wrapped her arms around the bottom
she couldn't keep her items
from falling through the box and onto the pavement.
This is not an allegory or another stupid poem.

II. POLYGONS OF VARIOUS COLORS

Bite Marks

I found bite marks on bark, which could've been the work
of only a yeti. The tree was still standing, yet leaned awkwardly
from the initial impact of the creature's jaws, carried forward
by the momentum of its massive body. I ran to tell my friend,
who I'd last seen circling a silver hexagon, also known as dread.
My buddy was nowhere, though, or at least nowhere nearby. To die,
after all, you just visit the next town over, where they serve blueberries
on lettuce with all their main courses. Being dead, of course, is
      like watching
your father circle a golden paradox while your hands sing tell me later.
      No one
has ever found a yeti corpse. There's a good reason for that.
      They live forever.

No need for sexual organs, thus no release of eternal lust. Even a tree
      will be dust.

Chestnuts

– C

Trees of Lawrence Kansas left the last dollar
for the man with the lime-green armband.
Oh I want all the little city girls to holler
for the sun-tanned farmhand in sweaty boxer
shorts. The wind blows the scrap of cloth
that hangs from the eaves of this house.
A wind blows the scrap of skin that hangs
from the leafy roof of my mouth. Wind blows
the scraps. Should've known this would end
in two sappy songs in a loop on a DAT
player playing through the night and sleep.
What's sadder than a forgotten cigarette left
to burn itself out? You call it a pout and a pose;
I call it blue-toned smoke clouds and ash
white sky. And don't forget the tan tar
smeared on our eyebrows. "You laugh when I tell
you you're gorgeous." Your eyebrows will never fall
out. You're gorgeous. The world is full of the sound
of lucky chattering squirrels. For inside your sex
there is a chestnut. And inside that there is the sun.

Proper Sycophant

The sun cannot melt concrete
The mosquito lives despite us – not a proper sycophant
Digital pictures do not fade and that makes me sad
Summer is meant to be wasted
I missed your call once every decade and it was enough
Do your hands hold water despite the glass that keeps the water in place –
    you are a proper sycophant
Depending on objects, we have always depended on objects
Roll that boulder over my grave I am not getting out
A guitar feeding back, a wash of vintage synth tones, underground music
    for underground people
The sound of dirt settling as seemingly insignificant insects more alive
    than us tunnel through it
Ask me in three hundred years if I like green beans and I'll have
    a different answer for you
Ask me if you look pretty in that dress and I'll say yes and yes and yes
Winter is meant to be spent wasted
In spring we drink the melting snow
In summer the honey knows no envy
The hummingbird stays afloat despite the breeze we displace
    as we approach it for a closer look-see
Fall is always pixelated in a poignant way
I miss today before it is even over
This has been my problem since I first said something concrete
Hold my hand, it's all I can ask
Tell me it's true, tell me it's true, tell me it's true

For My Son, Six

"When I conjure memories, they feel like someone else's" – even if
        the memory is
from just yesterday, or only five minutes ago. You opened up your hand
        to take
the saucepan I held out, and I ended up handing you a dachshund
        three days later.

It was a new morning when next I opened my eyes, but I had not slept yet.
        No wonder
I was tired of sitting around. On Tuesday, I watched Jesus let
        a five-year-old
                get run over
by a truck on the highway just outside my shack. He, in his omnipotence,
        was getting back at
the kid's dad for that bloody prostitute. You see, it all balances out,
        and never mind the theory of
relativity, which nobody really understands anyway. Of course, I cannot
        actually look at the Son
for his brightness, but His Handiwork is everywhere evident.

As a consequence, I turned away from the cross
and took up the study of karma. The whole thing makes sense now –
        go to the trouble of creating
a spark of light in the form of a child, then swallow it whole
        when the timer goes off for something
the one who is being swallowed has not even begun to gain
        knowledge of yet, let alone commit. Ding, you're dead,
you stupid little believer in Santa Claus.

I am holding out for a theory of post-irony. I am holding out
the hand of a dead relative. I am sorry for everything I have been forced
to forget. May the mini black hole I have created suck me in
and compact me into dusty quarks before it gets anywhere near you.

No Worries, Mate

A gun painted plum – a penlight shone
into the barrel would show some rust growing
in there. The gun pointed toward a rose bush –
moonlight cannot decide which petal
to reflect off, so douses them all. The shadow
of the gun's barrel falls between buds, obscures
only the ones that have dropped to the ground. I close
my mouth around the night air and savor the hurt
I taste there. The whole scene is a flow chart of shadow
and reflection – the sun pings off the moon's face,
filters through the clouds and bounces off every surface
to be found, all objects both casting and recasting
the original source. I lie down among the bush's roots. I know I am
what the sun uses to make shadows, but what does the sun reflect –
only its interiority like an infinite system of mirrors
facing each other and finally turning outward? But whence
the first spark of light that starts the glancing and allows sight
into the places where we hide our sallow faces? It all stops
when I swallow. The bullet has come from a barrel painted plum,
passed past rust, pierced several rose petals, and placed itself finally
in my bloodstream. It is now definitively red. Branch-shadows flit across
my cheeks and forehead, soggy blossom-piles lumpy under my back.
     I leak liquid light and love my eyes
are both open and closed. They reflect regardless.

Peer Pressure

Somebody pinned up glossy
full-color glamour headshots of male
investment bankers
on the walls of the office men's room stall.
Should I be worried that their smiles
do nothing for me or that I find
white collars on blue dress shirts
passé? The one with the gray hair
and green eyes makes it hard to care
whether the band
of my underwear is a little tight
as I stand over the bowl's water and try
to think of something other than a bunch
of smiling rich dudes watching me pee.
But I digress. What I really want to say is
the bathroom floor's a mess, hasn't been cleaned since
God knows when, and the maggots look hungry and frantic
as they circle the week-old carcass of a Prince Albert
tobacco can someone left there ten years ago.

Holy Succubus

I was changing in the locker room when the phone rang. The voice on the other end sounded vaguely female, wholly familiar, and called me by my name, "Hi Ron, I know it's been nearly four months, but I need to see you," followed by a dial tone.

I knew it was the pretty Asian-Italian woman with long black hair and absolutely perfect body. As the TV host Stephen Colbert would later go on to say, by way of describing just how perfect her body was, "You see, there are different kinds of mustard – French's yellow, ballpark . . ." The punch line, of course, concerned that elusive level above even Grey Poupon.

I could tell by the tone of the woman's voice that she wanted to sleep with me – if possible, right there in the locker room. To the best of my knowledge, I had never been introduced to her, nor had ever spoken a word in her presence. I wasn't even sure how she knew my name, not to mention remembering it after four months. Nonetheless, I looked around to see where we might be able to sneak off and enjoy each other.

When she arrived, she tried to convince me to accept the necessity of pain – to go beyond necessity even and begin to strongly desire pain as a means of growth or amusement.

She was fully clothed but already naked in the light of reality, and she lifted up her right forearm, turning it to show me her wound: It was black in the center, faded to pink toward the edges, looking somehow fresh yet ancient at the same time. The wound would clearly spread. She had made it herself, intentionally, like many of us did in junior high school with erasers as a sort of dare or contest. The wound only increased my desire to fuck her. I agreed with her wholeheartedly.

And woke up in a shadow.

The Rumble and Clatter of Underground Transportation

It was late afternoon by the time the plane took off. The sun hit us
from the side, the plane's shadow reflected on the clouds for a moment
before disappearing, and again a few seconds later on a different section
of the cloudbank, and after another minute on an entirely different cluster.

The plane's shadow then left for good, conditions changing as we climbed.
I could no longer see the people on the ground,
         though their handiwork was
everywhere evident. The plane replaced its shadow with itself,
         cutting through
the solid wisp, the scenery now subsumed.
                                    The flight attendant crushed each can
with his right hand. "It's easier that way," he said and smiled.
         From the last row,
I couldn't tell if anyone smiled back. The couple with the baby
         were sleeping.
From her father's arms, rising and falling with his breath, the baby
         was looking
around the cabin, calm, perhaps a bit bored with the general lack of color
and contrast. The bright light from the row of little television screens
         hanging
from the ceiling seemed to interest her for a moment or two. She looked
         at each
in turn down the line until the last one, whose screen was
         almost entirely blocked
by the receding squares of each that came before it.
                                    Why won't the young woman
in front of me, the curve of her upper arm visible through the gap
         in the seatbacks,
a magazine held in her simple and clean hands, turn the page
         from the story
about the Love Boat's Isaac?

She'd been on it for as long as
I had been looking,
her eyes open, lips silently forming the words as her eyes
traced them. The article
was just two paragraphs. The rest of the page was filled
with advertisements for Skoal
and Jergens lotion. Her lips kept moving, her cheekbone twitched slightly
with each "s."
Say the word
"smile." Go ahead – it doesn't need to be loud. Then tell me the clouds
look like bus exhaust.
I thought
it was a floater from my eye imposed on the horizon the clouds formed
with the pale sky in the distance,
but it was just a yellowish brown stain that had slid down the window
and gathered into a small globule
where its momentum and gravity had together given up.
I am trying to say
that this plane was all we had,
notwithstanding the photos in our pocketbooks and wallets.
The approach of night
was sped up by the fact we were flying east. The subways didn't matter
up here. I could almost hear them.

Pharmaceutically Jackknifed

An executively compensated vice president
of a medium-sized private equity firm, struggling
to remove the plastic wrap from a pack of Post-it notes –
this is just one of my favorite things.
                                       Don't bother with the airlift,
I am coming home. Wheezing in a cancer ward, strapped
to a small nuclear missile, I am coming home. Pulling the knife
from my own chest, forgiving my father for forsaking me,
        "the plane! the plane!" –
I am coming home.
                        A pharmaceutically jackknifed boot salesman,
        holding his breath
for the fortieth time today, as his fortieth customer of the morning
        slips off her pink UGGs,
stretches and sighs – one more of my favorite things.
        An anonymous participant
in a double-blind clinical trial undertaken to prove the efficacy
        or otherwise
of a new solar-powered helmet for migraine relief, grimacing,
        but not from the helmet
or the migraine – yes, a favorite.
                        Hold me I am bleeding
        from the hippocampus, my urges are
no longer my own, I am coming home. The fetid water is up to
        the third floor now, my hands
hold tomorrow's hamburger today with pickles on top,
        my mind remembers – I am coming home.
A thirty-nine-year-old man whose heart is sagging, struggling
        to remain upright as the plain
of the ground beneath him tilts first imperceptibly to the left
        and then all the way right, night's bane,
dew as day's pre-cum – our favorite things as antidotes, I am coming
        home, reserve the morning.

III. CONTAINERS

Halloween with the Future Child

It doesn't take a lot of time
       to learn to make the rhymes
                      fall
in the right places. Nor how
       to write a pleasing pentagram iamb.
Off-rhyme is like a book that refuses to be turned
       into a dachshund.
              All in all
I learned to like alliteration.
                  I asked
dissonant forms to hang out for once with as-
       sonant antfarms.
            But the charms have started to bore
me.
       I want to make something sloppily
eternal, more cleanly
       beautiful – a hand-me-down-
           turned smile, the mouth of my beautiful wife
              somehow lighting in
                 our child's sad pumpkin-
face someday.
          Lilies and orchids are temporarily
      morbid, then their petals fall off
into glory; the hand decides
      the knife's fate.
          Our work
           leaves us
               grinning.

M...S...G...

A man cracks open his fortune cookie, reads
he will walk into a hole with a thin skin
of earth covering it and not lose his hat. He's
thinking about this for several decades when

he realizes it is time to ask the woman what
hers reads. He asks. She says she has
a secret desire to be the hat. "But is that
the fortune?" he asks. "Sure, at least it was

when I read it centuries ago." The company that sells
them, though, got the distribution ratios all wrong.
Instead of printing several hundred fortune tellings

for a town of several thousand, each strip should say
the same thing: *Time on earth will be unbearably long,*
though it will take only a quick crack to fall away.

My Mom's House Has Been Cold for Years

He's always hitting her with his right hand.
On their left hands they wear wedding bands.
"Are you the trash it left behind?"
What will make her change her mind

and leave him to circle his sadness alone
and continue to cultivate inside his stone
of emptiness? He feels with his right hand.
She wanted nothing more than to dance

and have some good times and fun.
For her it's always a hidden sun.
For him it's wind and storm clouds,
a voice in his head, too loud,

making it hard to hear his feelings
sing and feel entirely his raw being.
He's afraid to be alone in the world.
They both resent she's not a little girl.

Now she's caught in a trap.
Her new kitten lies in her lap
and provides the only tenderness
to counteract her eternal sadness

in a house that's just silent and cold.
She's always feared it – now she's old.

A Red Dream Leaving

Why make the little girl leave somebody's red dream?
  It's too late.

Why does somebody dream the little red girl leaves?
  It's too late.

Why does the dream leave the little girl with somebody red?
  It's too late.

Why make a red dream the little girl leaves with somebody?
  It's too late.

Why does the little girl somebody dreamed was red leave?
  It's too late.

Why does somebody's dream leave the little girl red?
  It's too late.

Why dream the little girl leaves somebody red in his dream?
  It's too late.

Why make somebody's little girl dream of red?
  It's too late
    to leave it.

A Flock of Seagulls

We flew. We were flying. We did fly. We had flown. We have flown.

      We fly. We are flying. We do fly.

            We will fly. We will be flying. We will have flown.

      We fly. We are flying. We do fly.

We flew. We were flying. We did fly. We had flown. We have flown.

IV. WALNUTS

In Other Words

You are standing outside.
A thick rope hovers above
the ground and recedes
an infinite distance away from you
toward and then beyond the horizon.
Coming toward you it proceeds just above
your shoulder and past your right ear
disappearing an infinite distance
behind you. Along this rope at fairly regular intervals
there are knots, which represent
the life of each being who has been, is, or will be
including your own past and future lives (if you believe
in that kind of thing). The knots beyond the horizon are
the dead folks. The knots you can see are your fellow
breathers. And the knots behind your back – well, use
your imagination. The question: Given the infinite recession
and procession of this rope, and given that it is a single
unbroken rope, how were the knots tied? The basic fact
of your existence requires a profound suspension of disbelief.

The Morbid Autobiographer

– After Cioran

It is no sign of benediction to have been cheered by a disregard for the saints. This seeming cheer is tainted by a weak and vague hope for health and a choice of sexual congress that is made from an unconsidered perception of the prevailing morale climate or from a sense of what you can get away with, rather than from a firmly rooted understanding of the need for ecstasy. You are easily encouraged in sanctity only if you have never been disappointed by the heavenly paradoxes; having been disappointed, you turn to yourself, of a familiar purport, imbued with known stenches and falsehoods; you put your hopes in logical undertakings grounded in everyday sensations, solid, upstanding work with a comforting worldliness, the occasional thrills of the mistress, exercising just enough to avoid triple bypass, believing in the certainties of science; and so you avoid the saints, their ability to work without hands, their absence of desire to make themselves ostentatious, their homelessness. Typical halfhearted subsistence! You carry on respectably until your death, no need to think about it, suspending your disbelief for the sake of movie heroes because they may well be fantasy but at least you can see them in widescreen holding things. Behold the pessimist turned autobiographer, planting his flag in the graveyard. . . . He plants it even though he is starting to suspect his coffin is more like a customs office than a final destination. Nothing in heaven is easy, not even sanctity, and it won't be necessarily appointed – but it can be. . . .

I Pity the Poor Fools

When I was a small girl, I thought my pants smelled
like the skin underneath them. Now, as a grown woman
I realize they smell like something deeper than skin.
No matter how many times I wash them, they won't lose
this human stink. And to think, I once blamed it all
on something soft and supple, sensitive.
                                    Our smell
will someday leave the world along with us. What will
the next unlucky fuckers smell like? Will they sweat?
Will they have two noses?
                        Did the last boy brontosaurus miss
the last girl brontosaurus' scent when she wandered off
lost to wherever she went?
                        Some days I'd like to follow her there
and wait for the new stink. Oh how I wish I could be there
with my cute little button nose. The only old lady luckily left
to start a new race with unlucky new fucks who'll think
I'm rad avant-garde, wanna make me just to see what pops out,
never realizing how everyday and drab I once was.
                                            I'd sew my nose
on the flies of their orange jeans just to keep them from nakedness;
I'd sniff their dirty thingamajigs, shaped like nothing I can think of
right now, but probably smelling like a combination of cornflower
and old tires or something. We're all always made of oldness,
even the new unlucky fuckers. We need a big can of Endust!

An Endless Rope of Licorice

Everything is disappearing and you
are disappearing. Lips are solid
and give. There is no there is no
there is. There is just night and the way
its cars on the highway and the casual voices
trailing by the window sound
so far away. They are on the edge
of your disappearing
along with your self. And sound
waves
then travels forever. For example
the sound of this mechanical
pencil on this clean white sheet of paper
goes on forever and always
out
from itself like this
disappearing.
And we.

Cotton Candy

We're all cotton candy
spun by God
for no other reason than to be eaten
by smiling children
wearing multicolor wristwatches.

As fluff, how do we manage
to make one another shiver,
tremble, shudder, throb,
and generate more fluff
with such frequency?

Is it our sweetness? Our edibility?

The only cotton candy
that knows it is
cotton candy
we eat ourselves sick.
How hard it is to refrain
from lunging at each other
with teeth snapping.

Only children are human,
the rest of us are artificially colored
wisps of sugar.
In other words, capable of dissolving
into the air, which is composed
entirely of stomach acid and bile
when one is loveless and unsheltered.

Smiling child
how I miss you
tonight.

Her Red Dress Was Made of Her Blood

The shoe was empty so I poured a pint of milk
into it, until it reached the brim and overflowed
the rim where the foot goes through. It makes me
giggle, thoughts of my mom's birth canal. And then
I walked along the earth's canals and into the galaxy's
brightest flashlight bulb, radiating out and onto
and baking our skin into vitamin brown, and the body
sleeps sometimes too. My mother was soil. The thing that
really sucks is even if we could live forever, a couple of
C batteries would run out soon enough anyway, even
on the cosmic scale. And so the milk would overflow
a predictable amount of time longer and then would freeze
onto the carpet, creating a particularly smelly mess before
the springtime that won't come. We cannot just build a new
one. When you say a melon is ripe to mean it will taste real good,
and also say the corpse is ripe to mean it has been sitting awhile
and has begun to stink real bad, you will be saying the same thing.
If the ladder's top rung breaks while you are trying to leap beyond it
and you end up laid up for awhile in traction, the melon will go bad
pretty quickly even in the refrigerator. (Cite: Walt Disney.) In tribute
however to my mother I hearken back to the soil and reinsert the seed
from which we all will eat until the bleeding batteries run out. I've seen
the ads. They say Coppertop. They say Everlast. They say Energizer.
      They say over and over.
I say nighty night night. In tribute however to my father I say
thank you for holding the flashlight so steadily in Virginia's eternal night
woods. Christ was Dionysus For Dummies. Available now from IDG
are others: They say Sowing For Dummies. They say
      Harvesting For Dummies.
I've seen the ads. They say Wonder Bread. They say Buttertop.
      I say it's the same
flaming grains over and over again. It's tasted that way for millenniums.

It's the beauty of Christ

and the sadness of an empty shoe. I married my wife so we could have
       a few

babies, and fuck a lot. We'll have time to rot while we freeze to death.
       Us too.

We've seen the ads. They say Nike Nike Nike. They say just do it.
       They say seven

green and victory. I say um, excuse me . . .

Maps and Legends

When we die, perhaps we don't really see God's face, but our own face
for the first time. Think about it, you have never seen your face.
      You will never
see your face while living. Although maybe those who have had
      a near death experience
have seen their face, come to think of it. Is that part
      of the reassurance
upon coming back to life, that the face has been independently verified
      to exist, by one's own
self no less? Some people refer to their face as a "map." The question,
      of course:
How do you find your way in life, if you can't even see the map?
      Have you ever tried
to navigate a tricky terrain while holding a map up to a mirror?
      You would end up
going the wrong way half the time. It's a miracle we ever end up
      getting anywhere.

In a Beginning . . .

So, a big bang happens. Particles scatter for eons, but eventually formations begin to adhere and cohere, the number of potential configurations increases steadily during the expansion. At a precise moment, complexity reaches the breaking point at which every possible combination of atoms and circumstances has been achieved, followed by a collapse and lengthy dissolution/contraction. Then dormancy.

And start again.

After each big bang, you are born in one time and place along the way. It could be during the expansion or during the contraction. How will you know? Due to the randomness inherent in the system, your exact combination of atoms may be born in the Roman empire or a future China, rather than in the current United States that you hold so dear. (By that token, your current spouse might be born in ancient Egypt next time, while you end up hanging out with the pilgrims in America later in the cycle – you will miss him/her deeply without even realizing it.) You recognize some people and will further unbreakable bonds with them, bonds that have been formed over the course of numerous post-big bangs. Most people, you don't recognize, and remain a stranger to them for multiple millennia. Given eternity, though, you will end up meeting everyone in every possible circumstance at some point, you just won't remember most of them.

A single cycle seems to take forever – it includes us for only, say, 1/1,000,000,000,000,000,000,000th of that particular time period. But what a 1/1,000,000,000,000,000,000,000th it is. Try to enjoy.

You won't remember the 999,999,999,999,999,999,999/ 1,000,000,000,000,000,000,000 eons in each cycle during which you don't exist in your eternal form. But they can't hurt you. Your atoms will safely inhabit some other being/object until your number is called again.

Airwaves

(((Thank God for the treble speaker.))) Her voice
radiates on and out into the farthest reaches
of space, and on and in ricocheting resonating
off the inside of our skin-walls, our organs

tuned by her perfect pitch. The matchbox is
never empty, struck match echoing. The sun
matches her voice most when it reflects off
the moon. She sings in empty spaces. She is how

kittens and cats purr. The table feels her breath flow
perfectly evenly through its legs and surfaces.
Face it. You'll need her quiet sound as comfort
when we are sleeping under ground or bundled

in plastic baggies in a blue-green candy tin.
We're *always* just sitting around doing nothing.
Pink noise while we're daydreaming *and* sleeping.
(((Thank God for the treble speaker.))) And her voice.

V. VENUS FLYTRAPS

Caress This Tree

A tree grows slowly;
the whole time it's lonely.
It feels every new millimeter
yet touches nothing other.

It yearns for spreading leaved branches
to entangle in another's leaved branches.

Its sap blood pulses up
seeking union with the sun.
Look, it's grown another inch.

It bends with its sadness
while it watches us couple sweetly.
Lets drop pinwheel seedlings.

They shoot to the warm soil
aching for the joys of sexual toil.

Ask Me in Three Hundred Years

By wintertime, leaves and fruit have disengaged from their host,
the tree, and completely disappeared, with no observable trace left.
In the springtime, though, out of this nothingness,
        this seemingly complete
absence of matter, the leaves and fruit reappear. Like trees, our souls
have unseen roots. The roots get entangled with the roots
        of each other tree.
Yet at that point of the continuum at which the surface is broken,
        each tree asserts
its unquestionable uniqueness. And though the current manifestation
        of our body is temporary,
and falls off and disintegrates, the process is only one stop
        in an eternal cycle. Our body
will remanifest itself – if it used to be an oak leaf, it will once again be
        an oak leaf; if it used to be
an orange, it will still provide vitamin C in its juice. Our bodies are
        parasites; the good news
is that we are also – and more so – the host. And that snowflake
        melting on your tongue is a ghost.

We No Longer Use the Word "Chapeau"

The way raindrops bounce off each other
and break as they fall
reform as new raindrops but still descend
collide with fellow water and break again
maintain a liquid wall all the way down
until hitting the ground and taking form
longer term as a puddle
or soaked-through red windbreaker

transformed a final time in ascension.

The collective scent of a thousand decomposing bodies
escapes through the skin of cemetery soil, making
each leaf of grass place a small handkerchief of carbon gas
over its nostrilly surface and recoil
before breathing out again the oxygen we need to start the mower.

The inner band of your chapeau is darkened by your sweat.

They are drilling for oil in my mother.
The doctor says $2.35 a gallon.
Laugh kookaburra, laugh.

We work the crowd
the microphone
our voice too loud
no longer fun
the jokes we tell
that awful smell.

My son has drawn a pretty picture of a guitar.
Do you want to hear it?

K

I am happy with the way the constant sunlight hangs
on the face of everything in this room right now. I am happy
with packages – how they're delivered by numbers. The drummer
hits the cymbal five times. That birdsong has seven steps up,
six down. He ate his cigarettes, filters and all, my friend Dave did.
"Oh I believe it's all because Daddy's payday is not enough."
When I was 10, I was happy with the way my zero hung off the one.
One day, I hope to add another zero to the same old one, as I blow out
a cakeful of candles – a faceful of smiles on my wrinkled pate.
The cat marks with significant patterns of musk the pieces of paper
piling up on the carpet. What number does my small intestine tell
       the colon
when it's time for yesterday's sustenance to head back out into the world?
How much is touch? And what number will whatever tell the sum that is
my body when it's time to make the final subtraction?

To find hope, let's keep counting
the steps in a bird's song, shall we, and listen for all our cells singing
in their harmonious, teeming voices. I can almost hear
       the bloody numbers
multiplying and dividing, the equations solving themselves. I am happy
with the way the constant sunlight hangs on the face of everything
       for now.

Ladder to the Bottom of a Great Lake Reversed

We live that's what I love best
and the sun shines down from above
to bake our pizza crusts
while they're still a part
of the earth.
                 Apart from this
I love when you go deep honey
receiver. You know when you feel it
in your reflective silver dime-width
nippletips. I have twenty cents

says Venus Mint makes all
God's coins equally beautiful.

By deep of course I'm referring to when
I'm way in. One of my favorite adjectives
has always been wet.
                    We take part in
this thing that also produces petals pink

and green and red with fragrant hummingbirds
when we lock in.
                      There is no need
for a metaphor incorporating seeds. At this point
it is necessary to enter the noun power. The sun.
The gerund. The sunshine resting alike on both of us.

And your skin is the flower. I am a stem
with earthen stamina from rooting around
the black trauma for an elevator up.
                      Dew as day's pre-cum.
It's ours.

Reverse Light from a Computer Screen

The nature of darkness is such that I cannot
tell the edge of my CD tower from the carpet
beneath and behind it. The nature of darkness

is such that shadows from my head and hand
fall onto this white page; body gets in the way
of light. The nature of darkness is such that I had

a fall – scuffed knees. The nature of darkness is such
that one minus one equals no one. The nature of darkness
is such that nouns later disappear into different forms

of themselves, which remain as factors, but the verb never
disappears. The nature of darkness is such that I suck
everything into my dirty center. The nature of darkness

is such that I empty heaven while I live; body gets in
the way of eternal light. The nature of darkness is such
that a crow eats only carrion. The nature of darkness is

such that the fetal position… The nature of darkness is such
that the eyes of a white lab rat close. The nature of darkness
is such that fetal flowering is fatal to the cord as well. The nature

of darkness is such that the subsoil root never even saw the petals
it produced. The nature of darkness is such that subconsciousness
doesn't even know what my mixed-up mind will do with its black-

inked words as the poem is produced into the light of a lightbulb. Later,
the nature of darkness is such that light from a computer screen forms
a black door against the backdrop of gray shadows in this room when
I look away.

The nature of darkness is such what the nature of darkness does. Bruises
on our knees from various things: It allows us to pray
       for a number of years
before we wake up undies on backwards. Blackbirds. Singing dead
                                       blackbirds.

Hell Angels

The fire crackles to tell me I am tree tonight,
warm in sappy skin,
ecstasy of branches creaking,
as I bend to feed Hell with my wooden hands.

The earliest regret I ever had was standing by a river
with nothing on but socks to keep me human.
Smell of bacon in the air. Boombox blaring
from the angry campsite next tent over.

Water takes forever to boil when your clouds are Angels.

Puddle Play

The tire hits the puddle. We hear
not only the initial displacement of water
but the sound the H_2O particles make
hanging in the air for a brief moment of stasis
before descent. When the displaced puddle finds
the ground, it sounds different than rainfall –
the distance traveled being much greater from a cloud,
an impact thrice as loud. The splash from a tire disturbs the soil
less. The rain offers more nourishment, but it all evens out.

It must be dusk.

Raindrops bounce off telephone wires one by one by
one, or rather they are momentarily displaced by the wires,
a brief sliding interruption. The child stands on the sidewalk,
not wearing a slicker, his hands red, his breath a nimbus
which will never fall but instead disperse uneventfully. When he breathes
in, how does he not drown? The air is so heavy. The atmosphere throbs
like the recordings NASA Voyager made on its way past Jupiter.

A total eclipse occurs every evening around this time. We wait for it.
        We enjoy it –
every atom in our body at rest and in balance, the blood hums
        rather than pulses. The night
that follows agrees with us less, if only because of our loneliness,
        no matter with whom
we share beers at the moment the sun disappears. We hold
        each other's hand; there is nothing
better than the texture of another's skin, so different from water, so thin
        to be holding in all our organs.

The Temple of Its Stomach Will Forget You

— After Steven Jesse Bernstein

I have always feared the chemical formula of the atmosphere
consists of stomach acid and bile.
                                        Pistachio crusted grouper
on a bed of coconut rice, pineapple compote on the side, Diet Coke.
It was a good meal and a special night, but most likely I will not
remember it a hundred years from now.
                                        The columns
holding up Its temple may crack the top of the sky and reach
an air never breathed by meat or potato, but It will forget you.

        I will not.

VI. LATTER DAYS

Sleepyhead

The fall is
useless
to me I
say
sifting through
the trash – a
pigeon.

Brackish

In a sterile beaker, add two hydrogen molecules to one oxygen molecule to make pure water.

Add two million hydrogen molecules to one million oxygen molecules – it's still pure water.

Now pee in the beaker.

The water remains water, but the chemicals of your urine are added – you still have exactly two hydrogen molecules for each oxygen molecule, but now you also have the molecules that your urine comprises in solution with the water.

In other words, although it's no longer only water in that beaker, the water is still water, pure in its essential being, a formula that abides.

The chemical composition of your pee includes the molecules of whatever you drank earlier in the day, which includes whatever chemicals the manufacturer used to make the soda pop, with sometimes a little spittle mixed in from whichever worker was pissed at his boss that day.

We could go on like this forever, further fouling the water.

The point is that the extra stuff affects the basic existence of water not at all.

Somewhere, water still exists in its pure state, waiting to solve everything.

–

I have no idea what the formula looks like for a human being in its fundamental state.

But I do feel confident that, just as H_2O equals pure water, before our parents fuck us up or the smog catches up to us in the form of liver spots, some other equally precise combination of molecules equals a pure human.

My neurons may misfire serotonin.

Your blood cells may get invaded by cancer cells.

But somewhere underneath it all, you and I are exactly the same person, an equation perfectly balanced on each side of an equals sign.

I am not sure whether this is a consolation – something to carve into a headstone.

When I am out of town, I know I miss my wife more than I miss the lady who serves me coffee.

Is love then nothing but a biochemical bias?

Labia folds feel like leaf buds between my lips.

Pretentious Glasses

We walk through the valley of the shadow
of death, which consists of our entire earth and all
the dark creatures and objects on and in it. And death is
the great unbearable, inconceivably bright and white
light that casts us down here like characters in the projected
stream of an old talkie on a tattered screen.
                                                    The dome lid is pried off
a little to give us a glimpse when the sun sets or rises, but its beam is just
a slanted speck of dust compared with the immense everywhere-/
        nowhere-ness
that is true vision, and offers only a simulacrum of the glorious freedom
        of death.

Fantod

His mom met his dad — one plus one became
two. His mom and his dad procreated him —
one plus one became three. What other word
for it is there than magic? He always chose
the smallest word possible to convey accurately
his sense of feeling. He liked us like that.
Sometimes, though, only one of the fancy words
would do the trick — his depth of feeling exhausted
the dictionary even.
                    In Berlin I see so many men
who remind me of him — the look of innocent yet
all-knowing curiosity willing to take in anything
and accept it as whole and holy just as it is,
maybe a ponytail, sometimes a beard, glasses
optional — but all these men him in some way.

Dear God it makes me so lonely he left us
like he did. "I can see him petting his dogs
and saying sorry." One minus one became
none that evening. It is simple arithmetic.
It is the opposite of magic. He would find
the right word for it. I won't even try. The word
remains unchosen. Our world became unchosen.
Hey there, nice bandana! Will you take it off for me?

Medical Tourism

Let down and hanging. A factory hum
in the jugular. A crimpled garden hose.
A puddle that lasts an hour. Fuck knows
how we misrecognize the ghost, watching
clouds gather. Without representation
in heaven, I wander down here. Misrepresent
a sentiment. Forget to write rhyming words.
All is forgiven in All Is For Giving In, Ohio.
You've got your good things and I've got
a canker sore. Time was, you could hear
the condensation in the radiator, a conversation
through the heating ducts. You will individuate,
but not just yet. The young man you used to be
is still handsome. To learn how to read advertorials
for a living, press 1. To learn how to tune a drum,
press 2. To learn why your boyfriend thinks you are ugly
and dumb, press 3. To learn how to have a good cum,
press carbon and salve the rope burns on your inner right
wrist. Tap-dancing businessmen in their hard-soled shoes
exit the bathroom while I piss. Fly shit on road-kill. Erector
sets. Lincoln logs. Hasbro balls. Gyroscopes. Cap guns. Sparklers.

Lady with the Stroller You Have a Beautiful Baby

All the beauty in the world is not enough. Pigtails,
flannel shirt open to the navel, my semen drips
from her chin onto the collar of her shirt, she looks up
and smiles. It is not enough. An A-minor chord
is slowly absorbed into an E-major 7, single note ostinato
pulses, the word *hope* chanted for an hour over top of this.
I wish it were enough. My seven-year-old son wants a hug
before I leave for work, his eyes as he makes the request
are close, very close, but not enough. Floating amidst
Saturn's rings, harvesting ice, the light in the distance seems
to approach, I yearn for its warmth on my control panel,
even as I realize it is an optical trick that makes it seem
like it's coming closer. I want union with whatever God represents,
I need contact that would never be close enough – the emptiness
at the center of every atom of my being assures this. A dust bunny
crouching patiently in the corner of the living room watches me
as I grasp at everything no less futilely than its own slow gathering.
"The birds in the trees singing our mobile melodies." What a sweet,
sweet world indeed we leave behind us. No wonder Orpheus looked back.

Apple Cores

He started with model airplane
glue, proceeded to acetaminophen
with codeine, a triple
dose. The blueberry cereal bar had sat
open in its box for who knows
how long. The corner closest to the tear
in the wrapper had become more dense than the rest
of the bar. He added wet to the mix. The portion
of the cereal bar that had hardened still reminded him
of a gangrened limb. Again with the airplane glue, a sharp
knife, more scars for the future. In addition, there was something wrong
with the red Teletubby. It had smiled down at him from the screen.

Super Boring Marketing Meeting

Sat so long on the ottoman
the drool had dried crispy
in my beard. Makes a little
sound when my jaw moves
inadvertently. You see I talk
to myself, but only on accident.
You watch me through a window;
on occasion you cry. Wipe away
the tears before they can dry
in the shallow creases near your lips.
We are different from each other
in this way. Within my field of vision
there are forty-seven cracks
in the wallpaper on the west-facing
plaster. A new one will emerge
while I watch. Each crack appears
of a sudden, fully formed. "Must remain
vigilant," spoken under my breath.

Three's Company

"I was afraid I'd eat your brains." The tax and benefits lawyer
made it quite clear he was just a regular guy. When it rained
I put the packets of self-help powder in the nightstand drawer
and got high instead. I no longer do drugs. I gargle Novocain.

A Kleenex will end up torn at some point in its life cycle. A smile
is worn once and never again. The car broke down, forty-seven pieces.
The local shaman was out of glue, so I swept the shards into a pile
and threw them in the dustbin, on which I set the lid. One of my nieces

had such nice fillings I forgot the topic at hand. I just kept nodding
and tried not to look in her mouth. The pink plastic plate was piled
with flowers, none of them of the edible type. They looked rotten
anyway. I reached out to touch a breast but missed it by a mile.

I am trying not to remember what else happened that day. Oh yes,
I made a list in two columns. One side was headed: <u>Reasons
to "Hang in There"</u>. Like my father on holiday, I never got a tan.

I was too busy trying to avoid spilling ketchup on my sundress.
I counted everything in fours: chugs of milk, changes in seasons,
the square in which I was caught. I thought I'd rather be a man.

Good Things Come in Threes

You can't fuck
a dog up
the ass with-
out a lit-
tle lubri-
cation and
that requires
premedi-
tation God
help us all.

Stopgap

What happened to the large pile of flags we used to keep
in a corner of the armory? The ones with 50 green dollar signs
on an orange background in the lower-right-hand corner, thirteen
black and white stripes alternating across the main body? Did I suffer

much? Does anyone give a shit about this poem if even I won't?
Let's start over: My solar plexus tingles at all times in anticipation
of loss. It doesn't matter what loss or of whom. It's not a matter of if.
I used to believe Jesus died for our sins so that we may rise again. Now

I believe Jesus died because he was convicted of committing crimes
against the state and so was strung up like they used to do in such cases.
The communion wafer was at one point a scattering of seeds. I don't need
any more of a miracle of transubstantiation than that. I'm sorry you do.

Yet dinner never seems to fill me up, so I keep eating all freaking night
until I can barely move, lying there on the sectional watching baseball
with the sound off, black metal in my earbuds, tears that just won't come
because I no longer feel enough to conjure them. The little rubber things

that tie back my wife's hair will last a hell of a lot longer than
              my wife's hair.
Robin Hood couldn't have cared less about what was fair
              in terms of wealth;
he simply enjoyed the redistribution of valuable things. I believe God
              also enjoys
such a redistribution, as Kyron's molecules help the weeds grow
              through the cracks

of whatever basement he ended up slaughtered in. It's all about balance,
              right? But what
is the corresponding joyful event for what happened to that kid?
              It all seems
pretty damn cock-eyed to me. "FTW" says the tattoo across the three

knuckles left
on the right hand of the guy who used to work at the sawmill (hardy har,
yuck yuck).

I make all this up as I go. I make all this up as I go. I make all this up
as I go. I make up
a stupid flag to begin a stupid poem because I don't know what else to do.
I am at a loss.

Silence Is Dead, Lee

I am sitting in
a soundproofed room
perfectly still
right
in front of
a large amplifier

contact microphone tacked
to my forehead
wired to the amp
turned
all the way up

hold my breath

blood pulses
a rhythm

wait for my brain
sounds
to feed back.

It Bears Repeating

A dust
bunny
crouching patiently
in a corner of
the living room
watches me grasp at
beauty
no less futilely
than its own
slow
gathering.

Thanks

Steve Jost

Bob and Ingrid Jost

Ryan Dewey

Nancy Zafris

Bill Nalley

Richard Bowering

About the Author

Ron Jost received his B.A. in writing and philosophy from the University of Pittsburgh. He also attended the Key West Literary Seminar's Writers' Workshop Program with John Ashbery, who referred to one of the poems in this collection as "beautiful" (ten bucks to the first person who guesses which one). Jost lives in Willoughby, Ohio with his wife and son.